D1252872

THE FREUD ANNIVERSARY
LECTURE SERIES
THE NEW YORK PSYCHOANALYTIC
INSTITUTE

FREUD ANNIVERSARY LECTURE SERIES

The New York Psychoanalytic Institute

DREAMS
AND THE USES OF
REGRESSION

Bertram D. Lewin, M.D.

INTERNATIONAL UNIVERSITIES PRESS, INC.

New York

Lecture held at The New York Academy
of Medicine on May 22, 1957

Contents

Note

THE FREUD Anniversary Lectures were established in 1951 to celebrate the birthday of Sigmund Freud and for the advancement of psychoanalysis, the science he created and to which
he devoted his life.

Beginning with this volume the Freud Anniversary Lectures will be published annually under the imprint of the New York Psychoanalytic
Institute.

The previously held and published Freud
Anniversary Lectures were the following:

1951 Rudolph M. Loewenstein, M.D.
      Freud: Man and Scientist[1]
1952 Ernst Kris, Ph.D.
      *Psychoanalysis and the Study of
      Creative Imagination*[2]

[1] Published by International Universities Press in collaboration
with The New York Psychoanalytic Institute, New York, 1951.
[2] *Bulletin of the New York Academy of Medicine,* Second
Series, Vol. 29, No. 4, pp. 334-351, April, 1953.

NOTE

1953 Phyllis Greenacre, M.D.
Psychoanalysis and the Cycles of Life[3]
1954 Anna Freud, LL.D.
Psychoanalysis and Education[4]
1955 Lionel Trilling, Ph.D.
Freud and the Crisis of our Culture[5]
1956 Ernest Jones, M.D.
The Nature of Genius[6]

[3] *Bulletin of the New York Academy of Medicine,* Second Series, Vol. 29, No. 10, pp. 796-810, October, 1953.

[4] An abstract of this lecture appeared in *The Psychoanalytic Study of the Child,* Vol. 9, pp. 9-15. New York: International Universities Press, 1954.

[5] Boston: Beacon Press, 1955.

[6] In: *Sigmund Freud: Four Centenary Addresses.* New York: Basic Books, 1956.

Dreams and the Uses of Regression

BERTRAM D. LEWIN, M.D.

Dreams and the Uses of Regression[1]

AROUND the year 500 B.C., natural science began with a repudiation of the dream. Heracleitos of Ephesos issued a scientific manifesto in the two sentences: "We must not act and speak like sleepers, for in our sleep too we act and speak," and, "The waking have one world in common, but the sleeping turn aside each into a world of his own." Professor Schrödinger, from whose chapter "On the Peculiarity of the Scientific World View" I am quoting these fragments, explains their importance. People were accustomed, then, he says, to treat what we now call the manifest content of dreams as valid perceptions; that is, they believed that the persons and things they saw in dreams were real. They thought, for example, that gods must exist because they appeared in one's dreams. When therefore Heracleitos referred to the world that

1 The title is phrased thus to recall Ernst Kris.

[11]

is common to all men, he meant the world of waking life; and in another fragment he specifically stated that whosoever does not recognize the world in common is not of sound mind but insane, and that he acts and speaks like a sleeper. We as psychiatrists and students of the dream thus have an ancient reason for great pride—at least a great negative reason. For at the very dawn of science, the dream and the psychologic symptom were such nuisances that science could not begin until they were explicitly expelled from scientific consideration.

Leaving Heracleitos, let us leap from 500 B.C. to 1952 A.D. and to Professor W. Ross Ashby. In his book, *Design for a Brain,* Ashby gives a clear and careful statement of what must be excluded from physical science—which is, generally speaking, consciousness. When we exclude consciousness from science, and in his context, from the observable functions of the brain, we do not, he says, deny its existence. "The truth is quite otherwise, for the fact of consciousness is prior to all facts." Here Ashby is referring to consciousness in the sense of subjective experience; for he continues: "If I perceive, am aware of, a chair, I may later be persuaded by other evidence that the appearance was produced by a trick of lighting; I may be persuaded that it occurred in a dream or even that it was a hallucination; but there is no evidence in existence that could persuade me that my awareness itself was mistaken—that I had not really been aware at all. This knowledge of personal awareness, therefore, is prior to all knowledge."

Why then must one exclude not only the dream consciousness but also the waking consciousness from one's thinking if one is to design a brain? Ashby echoes Heracleitos: "The answer, in my opinion, is that Science deals, and can deal, only with what one man can demonstrate to another. Vivid though consciousness may be to its possessor, there is as yet no method known by which he can demonstrate his experience to another. And until such a method, or its equivalent is found, the facts of consciousness cannot be used in scientific method."

The metaphysical assumptions of Heracleitos and Ashby are related but different. The Greek philosopher warns us against trusting our perceptions, especially those that come in sleep. The English scientist throws out all qualities of self-observation, even the raw stuff of waking common sense, as well as mirages, hallucinations and dreams. I think we must recognize the propriety of Ashby's working assumptions; how-

ever, it is difficult not to be wistful in regard to
one matter: because of his adherence to the
rules of scientific method, Professor Ashby will
be prevented from telling us whether the brain
he has designed can dream. Heracleitos, appar-
ently, was content to say that the manifest dream
content does not mirror an objective reality,
that *Träume sind Schäume.* Ashby, for the sake
of preserving scientific method, must not men-
tion dreams as objects of investigation. I do not
know precisely what metaphysical complications
would arise if the designed brain, built by some
science-fiction super-engineers and given a
chance to talk, should begin to tell its dreams.
I presume we should rule them out from science
too, though I can think of other science-fiction
possibilities. Nevertheless, as the physical sciences stand, or stood yesterday, the only function of consciousness is to observe and to perceive; the observer as a dreamer or self-observer
is out of the scientific world picture.

Professor Schrödinger is authority for the
statement, that this retreat of the observer from
the world picture is one of the basic metaphysical principles of the scientific view of the world.
He calls it "the hypothesis of the real world
around us" or "objectivation." He defines *objectivation* as the "exclusion of or dispensing

with the cognizing subject (from the understandable world-picture aspired to), who steps back into the role of an external spectator." I, my ego, am supposed to be there as if I were totally detached, a spectator. This philosophic point of view is called dualism; there is perceiving mind and objective matter, or, in Descartes' original statement, two kinds of things or substances: the thing that knows (*res cogitans*) and the thing that has extension in time and space (*res extensa*).

Schrödinger elaborates: "The scientist, almost inadvertently, simplifies his problem of understanding Nature by disregarding or cutting out of the picture to be constructed, himself, his own personality, the subject of cognizance. Inadvertently, the thinker steps back into the role of an external observer." Elsewhere the same author repeats that the scientific point of view is "cutting out oneself," "stepping back into the position of an observer who has nothing to do with the whole performance." The idea of the scientist as a purely observing, almost a purely looking, ego is to be found in all serious discussions of the metaphysics of science. Thus Professor Burrt, in *The Metaphysical Foundations of Modern Physical Science:* "Man is but a puny and local spectator" in the Newtonian picture of the world, and elsewhere he uses the phrase, "irrelevant spectator." These quotations and many others that could be adduced indicate that somewhere during the 2500 years between Heracleitos and Ashby, a great deal more was eliminated from science than the mere delusive testimony of manifest dream contents. The three great names associated with the scientific world view that made the spectator irrelevant are Galileo, Newton and Descartes; and Descartes was its formulating philosopher.

Descartes explicitly stated that the mind has "no relation to extension or dimensions" and that "we cannot conceive of its occupying space," but it is important to note Professor Burrt's remark, that in popularizations, and more particularly in those based on Hobbes's writings, the mind came to be thought of in space. In nonmetaphysical circles, it somehow gravitated to a location in the head, so that by Newton's time, "it is safe to say . . . the soul was conceived as occupying a seat, or a small portion of extension, within the brain, which place had come to be known as the sensorium." Like the little upsidedown man along the fissure of Rolando that we learned of in school, who became in modern parlance our "body image," a little observing homunculus inhabited the pineal gland, floated in the fourth ventricle, or sat near the crossing of the optic nerves, a weightless creature, kinsman of Descartes' other homunculus, the Cartesian diver. This *res cogitans* had only one function, that of the sensorium—to take in all impressions that came in from the organs of perception, one supposes mainly from the eyes.

In this somewhat sketchy version of the Cartesian view of mind and matter, or mind and body, the mind is a small purely cognitive *res;* it is reduced to spectatorship; even the body to which it is somehow related becomes a part of the outer world, for it can be seen "out there" in extension. Descartes thus separated observing mind and extended matter. We are told of precursors for this point of view among the early Greek philosophers. Descartes was soundly grounded in their writings, and they may have impressed him very much, but his own opinion as to the event most influential, indeed, portentous in shaping his thoughts was the dreaming of three dreams on the night of November 10, 1619. If his opinion is correct and to be taken seriously, we come upon a strange situation. The dream, rigorously excluded from the natural science world, for different reasons, by scientists from Heracleitos to Ashby, would be

[17]

the very source of the world view from which it was excluded. One aim of the present essay is to muster the possible evidence for this idea, and to suggest that what began as a dream experience may have determined the Cartesian scientific view of the whole world. The stone the builders rejected may have become the cornerstone.

To be perfectly direct about the matter, I shall try to show that Descartes' dualistic view of the world is the view that we commonly find in an ordinary well-projected visual dream, where the dreamer is exactly what the observer is supposed to be and tries to be in the Cartesian system, that is, *res cogitans,* the pure and irrelevant spectator, the external observer. In such a dream, the dreamer is all observer, and he does not directly feel himself as body in the dream picture, where he is represented only by projected images. In dreams of a different character and in certain going-to-sleep visual imaginations, the body may itself be felt in the dream picture; in these dreams that include body sensations, sleep is lighter, the disturbers of sleep more effective in waking the sleeper completely or partly; and in this sense, dreams with much body in them are not satisfactory as guardians of sleep. However, in those dreams which suc-

[18]

cessfully exclude stimuli from the body, the dreamer is there only with what Federn calls "mental ego feeling."

In fact, the psychoanalytic literature contains a very Cartesian discussion of the relation of the dreamer as the dreaming spectator to himself as a bodily participant, in Federn's study, "Some Variations of Ego Feeling" (1926). Federn there distinguishes what he calls "mental ego feeling" from "bodily ego feeling," according to where and what the dreamer feels himself to be. I think it would be possible to simplify Federn's terminology for our present purpose and to speak in the context of this lecture of mind and body. Indeed, to explain what he meant by mental ego feeling, Federn said that it was the observer in the dream, and he added, "The phrase, *cogito ergo sum,* is a rational formulation of mental ego feeling." I think that with this phrase, Federn is returning the Cartesian idea to its place of origin, namely, the dream. My existence *qua* dreamer has in the dream the same validity as my existence in waking life *qua* cogitator. *Somnio ergo sum.* Most dreams are, in the optical sense, projected and appear as if before us in our visual field, so that we readily understand the idea of spectator and dream picture. We are observers only and remain without bodily feelings, which disappear as we go to sleep.

In certain less frequent dreams, however, the body is felt intensely. These are dreams of flying, swimming and the like, certain anxiety dreams, and dreams of inhibited movement; and they are signs of physically disturbed sleep. Dreams vary in their capacity to overcome such intrusions from the body and differ in the extent to which they can delude the sleeper into believing either that he is not feeling or that he is feeling something else.

A few examples will clarify this statement. Freud records a dream where a poultice between the legs of a sleeper, who was suffering from an abscess in that region, became in the dream picture a saddle and the dreamer an equestrian. Scherner reports a dream which represented dental irritation by two rows of fair-haired boys attacking each other. I may refer to a comparable dream of dental irritation from my own practice: the dreamer found himself in the House of Lords. The Lords were seated not in rows but in a semicircle, the dreamer was at the center of the circle. Suddenly a very large rubber axe blade chopped down between two of the Lords on the right, and the dreamer awoke to find an irritating fragment of food between

two teeth of his lower jaw in an exactly corres-
ponding position. While the dream lasted, the
teeth had been projected out into the dream
world as Lords and had not "belonged" to him.

The following dream illustrates variations in
the representations of different parts of the
body. The dreamer fell asleep sitting upright in
bed and holding a book in his left hand. In the
beginning of the dream, from which he woke
immediately, he felt his shoulder and neck
muscles under great strain, as he heavily tried
to pull himself up a steeply inclined sidewalk.
He was intensely aware of the weight of his head
and shoulders, less so of his chest, and not at all
aware of any part of him from the waist down.
He was thus perceiving the actual state of the
musculature used to maintain his sitting-up
position. As to his left arm: on the left in the
dream, the middle of the street was full of lively,
rapid horse-and-buggy traffic. Awaking, he
found in place of the street, his left arm shaking
in a clonic effort to keep the book in its raised
position.

Such dreams are relevant in illustrating the
way the body is represented in dreams under
such special circumstances. They show that
parts of the body which are as if still awake may
appear in such a dream, and that they may be

felt then exactly as they would be if the dreamer were awake, or the visual images may delude him into believing that something else and not his body is responsible. Since the dream's main function is to preserve the dreamer's sleep, we may assume that the part of the dream related above, in which the tingling of the left arm is transmuted to street traffic on the left and in which the dreamer has no direct experience of his arm, is guarding sleep better than the part that permitted the dreamer to feel the painful tensions of his neck and shoulders directly. In the terminology of Descartes, the preservation of sleep is best accomplished in those dreams where the dreamer is only *res cogitans,* that is, mind, and not also *res extensa,* that is, body; unless of course there is too much cogitation.

We are now ready to get back to Descartes himself, for the philosopher had an unusual dream, one into which his body entered in a very spectacular way. The dream and two that followed on the same night made a deep impression on him. He was convinced that they were a revelation from God, and later he told them often and always spoke of them as marking the decisive point in his career (Burrt, p. 106). He said that they had brought him illumination and the complete conviction that mathematics was the sole key needed to unlock the secrets of nature. If we find a way to understand Descartes' profound conviction, we may possibly learn how he came to set up his dualistic world, a world, moreover, in which all that was physical was reduced to the three fundamentals of time, space, and matter.

The three dreams of November 10, 1619 have been published twice in the psychoanalytic literature, once in French as a footnote to a letter of Freud, and once in an essay of Professor J. O. Wisdom, which appeared in the *International Journal of Psycho-Analysis* in 1947, titled, "Three Dreams of Descartes." Descartes was twenty-three years old at the time of the dreaming, and the surviving account is due to his first biographer, Baillet. The text used here is from the translation by Professor Norman Kemp Smith in his book, *New Studies in the Philosophy of Descartes* (1952).

> Descartes tells us that, on November 10, 1619, having returned to rest full of enthusiasm and entirely taken up with the thought of having discovered the foundations of a science so marvelous, he had in a single night three consecutive dreams which he imagined could only have come from on high. After he had fallen asleep his imagination was strongly impressed with certain phantoms

which appeared before him and terrified him in such wise that, while walking, as he fancied, through the streets, he was obliged to turn himself over to his left side so as to be able to advance to the place where he wished to go, feeling, as he did, a great weakness in his right side which disabled him from leaning on it. Ashamed of walking in that manner he made an effort to straighten himself, but felt an impetuous wind which, catching him up in a kind of whirlwind, made him revolve three or four times on his left foot. But what really frightened him was something more; the difficulty he had in dragging himself along made him think he was falling at every step.

So far, we interrupt to note, this is an unusual dream. There is a great deal of bodily feeling in it, and Descartes is painfully aware of part of his own body's *res extensa* or matter. It corroborates Federn's assertion that the body is felt intensely in dreams of motion and inhibition of motion. Since this part of the text is the beginning of the dream, we may surmise that the dream work has not proceeded far from the waking state or the transition between waking and sleep where bodily sensations are still registered directly, of which the "tingling arm" dream above would be a good example. Descartes notes that when he awoke, he found himself lying on his left side, the side to which he felt himself turn

in the dream. As a guardian of sleep, this part of
the dream is not satisfactory; it may be con-
trasted with the one recounted above where the
representation of the teeth as the Lords, seen
but not felt, had successfully eliminated from
consciousness the concomitant dental irritation.
This is in accord with the general rule: the
more the dream thoughts can be turned into
purely visual representations, the more satisfactory and uninterrupted the dream.

To return to the dream:

> [He finally] perceived on his path a college
> with open gate [and he] entered, seeking there
> a refuge and a remedy for his trouble.

We recognize this type of dream element; it
is a "threshold phenomenon" like those first
described and so named by Silberer. In a dream,
going into another room and the like are signs,
according to Silberer, of a change in the dream
thoughts. My own alternative or additional interpretation of these elements is, that they indicate the appearance in the dream text of the
wish to sleep and a second try at forming a
dream that would eliminate its disturbers by a
new representation. Descartes' dream appears on
the face of it to permit this interpretation, although, as we shall see immediately, the attempt

was a failure. Whatever new thought may have arisen was one of defense—to get out of danger and distress.

The dream continues:

He tried to reach the church of the college, his thought being to go there for prayer, but perceiving that he had passed a man of his acquaintance without saluting him, he tried to return on his steps to make due acknowledgement and was flung violently against the church by the wind. At the same moment, he saw in the middle of the college court another person who called him by name in very civil and obliging terms, and told him that if he cared to go in search of Monsieur N., the latter had something to give him. M. Descartes imagined that it was a melon that had been brought from some foreign country. But what surprised him still more was to see that those who together with this person were gathering round him for conversations stood on their feet straight and steady, whereas he himself on this same ground was still bowed and staggering, and that the wind which more than once had been on the point of upsetting him had become less strong. With these imaginations in mind, he awoke . . .

Thus ends the second scene of the first dream, with the realization that his body was in distress and not the body or bodies of everyone. These terminal details of the dream demonstrate the reason for its failure to preserve sleep. Descartes found out that he was not able to project his sensations from himself—or perhaps his self from his sensations (Hartmann). The attempt at projection failed and he awakened.

As to the meaning of the dream so far, we shall later learn Freud's few comments concerning certain elements, such as the gentlemen and the melon. On general principles of universal symbolism, Wisdom has proffered more conventional suggestions in terms of sexuality. He thought that Descartes' body in the dream represented his phallos, that his struggle to stand up straight represented an effort to overcome impotence, that the violent wind was a castration threat, and that the retreat to the college church signified a flight to a protective mother. This interpretation at the infantile level may of course be correct, despite its generality. Yet it seems incongruous to attach so commonplace an interpretation to so unusual a dream.

We left the text of the dream at the words, "With these imaginations in mind, he awoke . . ."

> . . . he awoke and, as he did so, felt a pain that caused him to fear that all this was the work of some evil genius bent on seducing him. He turned at once to his right side, for it was on his left side that he had gone to sleep and had his dream. He

addressed a prayer to God begging to be protected from the evil effect of his dream and to be preserved from any misfortunes that might menace him in punishment for his sins, which, so he recognized, might be grievous enough to draw upon his head the bolts of divine vengeance—however irreproachable his life might hitherto have been in the eyes of men. In this situation, after an interval of nearly two hours passed in thoughts of various kinds on all the good and evil in this world, he fell asleep again . . .

In short, as he himself was to say later, he spent the two waking hours in a moral conflict. Descartes, Freud and Wisdom all agree that here *right* and *left* are used in the moral sense, as so often in dreams and symptoms. It is nevertheless worth considering whether Descartes' turning in bed was not also intended to relieve the tensions of his left side, which had felt so heavy in the dream.

To continue: After he had fallen asleep,

immediately there came to him a new dream, in which he believed he heard a sharp and piercing noise which he took for a clap of thunder, and opening his eyes, he perceived a large number of fiery sparks all around him in the room. This had often happened at other times; it was nothing very extraordinary for him to wake in the middle of the night and find his eyes sparkling to such a degree as to give him glimpses of the objects nearest him. But on this occasion, he chose to have recourse to reasons from philosophy; and after having observed by alternately opening and closing his eyes, the quality of the objects thus brought before him, he drew from it conclusions favorable to his understanding. Thus his fear was dissipated, and it was in a reasonably tranquil condition that he fell asleep again.

Descartes suggests later on in this account that his fright was remorse of conscience, and that the thunderbolt was a sign or portent, indicating that the Angel of Truth had come down to possess him. As for the lights, which he recognized as familiar, recurrent manifestations, I shall venture a plausible suggestion; namely, that they were flicker symptoms of an attack of some sort related to migraine or a convulsive condition. In support of this snap diagnosis, I suggest that the one-sided paralysis and the spinning felt in the first dream were experiences of the same attack. I have no idea why Descartes thought his flicker lit up the room. This may have represented an effort on his part to bring the phenomenon into line with the thunderbolt idea, as if the room had been filled by a flash of lighting; or Descartes may have been influenced by the pre-Newtonian theory of vision as a function that proceeded from the eyes on to objects; or it may simply be an attempt at projection; but the issue cannot be decided.

Another detail in Baillet's record also speaks for my hypothetical diagnosis, since it can be interpreted as indicating a prodromal intimation. When Descartes' friends wondered whether he had not drunk too much wine that evening, since it was Martinmas when heavy drinking was customary, he replied that he had not had a drop of wine for three months before the night of the dream, and "that the Genius which had been exciting in him the enthusiasm, with which, as he felt, his brain had been inflamed for several days, had predicted these dreams to him prior to his retiral to rest, and that the human mind had had no share in them."

Now, a premonition that one is to have a certain dream is something extraordinarily rare, if not completely unheard of. On the other hand, a premonition of migraine or a convulsive attack even several days before the event is relatively common. The statement therefore lends force to the idea that the dream was a psychic equivalent or accompaniment of such an experience, and that Descartes, during his sleep and on awaking from his second dream, had symptoms that we now believe are due to autonomous closed electrical circuits in the brain. The presence of such circuits was predicated many years ago, because of the paths taken by scintillations that accompany migraine headaches (it is pleasant to recall) by a member of this audience (Kubie, 1930).

To interpret the two dreams from the standpoint of the body sensations alone, we need only to repeat Freud's cardinal statement, that the purpose of the dream is to preserve sleep. To stay asleep, Descartes processed his physical symptoms into a struggle against the "impetuous wind." His use of the word *wind* reminds us that the word *aura* entered the language of medicine when a boy told Galen, that before his convulsions, he felt an *aura,* that is, a breeze, mount his body upward from his feet. Apart from any other determinations, we may postulate one meaning of the action of the dream, and one basic wish: Descartes wished to rid himself of his alarming bodily sensations in order to continue his sleep. He wished to sleep, and if he had to dream to do so, he wished to retain, as he might have put it, only his *res cogitans* and his position as a "detached and irrelevant observer." As to his painful *res extensa* and his bodily feelings, these he would be glad to banish and to project entirely to the insentient world picture of the dream.

To turn again to the account of this extraordinary night, we find that the third dream was
mild and agreeable. A moment after falling
asleep, he began his final dream,

> which unlike the two earlier dreams, had nothing
> terrifying in it. In this third dream, he found a
> book on his table, without knowing who had put
> it there. He opened it, and seeing that it was a
> dictionary, he was delighted, hoping that he might
> find it useful. At the same instant, he happened
> on another book, no less of a surprise to him than
> the first, not knowing how it had come to be there.
> He found it to be the collection of poems en-
> titled *Corpus Poetarum,* etc. Curiosity made him
> wish to read a little in it, and on opening the
> volume, he chanced to fall on the line *Quod vitae
> sectabor iter?,* etc. [Which path in life shall I
> pursue?] At the same moment, he perceived a man
> he did not know, who presented him with some
> verses beginning with the words, *Est et Non.*[2]
> These he recommended highly, insisting on the
> excellence of the poem. M. Descartes told him
> that he knew what the piece was, and that it was
> among the *Idylls* of Ausonius, one of the authors
> in the bulky poetical anthology on the table.
> Wishing to show it to the man, he began to turn
> over the leaves of the volume, quite certain of
> being perfectly acquainted with the order and

[2] Smith (p. 35) states that these two poems are on the same
page of the 1603 edition of the *Corpus,* and that they are face
to face on two pages of the 1611 edition. In both they come
under the eyes simultaneously.

general arrangement of the work. As he was thus searching for the place, the man asked him where he had got the book. M. Descartes replied that he was unable to say how he had come by it, but that the moment before he had been handling another, which had now disappeared, and all this without his knowing either who had brought it to him or who had taken it from him again. No sooner had he finished saying so, than he saw the book reappearing at the other end of the table. But he found that this Dictionary was somewhat different from what he had seen it to be the first time. Meantime he came upon the poems of Ausonius in the collection of poems he was handling and being unable to find the piece beginning with the words, *Est et Non,* he said to the man that he knew another passage of the same poet even finer, and that it began with the words, *Quod vitae sectabor iter?*

Because of the length and circumstantiality, I shall, for a moment, interrupt the story of the third dream. Psychoanalysts will be reminded by it of many they have heard, usually introduced by the dreamer's statement that he had an interesting dream. It will be of interest to you to learn, later on, Freud's opinion of this type of dream, for a psychoanalyst's tendency to be impatient during the telling of such dreams depends on a difference in aim between himself and the dreamer, which Freud points out.

However to continue the story about the books and the book-lovers,

> The person asked to have [the poem] shown to him, and M. Descartes was proceeding to look for it, when he came upon several small portrait engravings, and this caused him to remark, that the volume was very handsome, but that the edition was not the one he was acquainted with. He was at this point in his dreams, when both the man and the books disappeared, vanishing from his fantasy, without his yet awaking. What especially calls for remark is that, in doubt whether what he had just seen was dream or actual vision, not merely did he decide in his sleep that it was a dream, but he proceeded to interpret the dream prior to his awaking.

Before taking up Descartes' interpretation, it may be remarked that several others have commented on the dream. The suggestion of its alcoholic etiology, made by Descartes' friends, was refuted immediately by the dreamer himself; he had not drunk too much but had been completely abstinent. Other interpretations have come from Professor Wisdom, quoted above in passing, and from Freud. But since Descartes' priority of interpretation is so well established, we must first give his.

His account of the interpretation shows that

he was not interested in the analysis of the dream in Freud's sense; his interest was entirely anagogic, so that he may be regarded as a precursor of Silberer rather than Freud. He wished, in other words, to get away from his unconscious and to get into the field of moral and philosophical speculations, and to make an allegory of the dream. Thus, he said that the Dictionary in the third dream stood for all of the sciences, the anthology of poems for a union of philosophy and wisdom—for poets, due to the divine nature of inspiration, were often wiser than professional philosophers. The verse about the choice of a path in life represented a sage's advice, or possibly, moral theology. These ideas came to him while he was still asleep.

He awoke and, still meditating, interpreted the poets in the anthology as signifying "revelation and inspiration." *Est et Non* were the Yes and No of Pythagoras and referred to truth and error in human knowledge and the sciences. Descartes was so pleased by his success in fitting the pieces of the dream together, that he was convinced it was the Angel of Truth who had descended from Heaven to reveal to him the treasures of all the sciences. He could not find an explanation for the little copperplate portraits in the second book, but after an Italian artist visited him next day, he was satisfied and decided to look for no further explanation.

So much for Descartes' associations to the third dream, which was pleasant and which, he believed, bore on the future. The other two dreams, he believed, bore on the past, and they were admonitions from God. The melon he linked up, strangely, with the charms of solitude. The wind that thrust him toward the college and the church, he thought, was an evil genius trying to force him into a place he would have gone of his own accord, but which God did not permit. It was God, however, that made him take his first step toward the church. The terror of his second dream marked his remorse of conscience for sins he might have committed, and the thunder was the sign that the Angel of Truth had entered into him. After this, he prayed again to the Virgin, vowing to make a pilgrimage to her shrine at Loreto, part of the way on foot and clad in lowly garb. This vow was fulfilled only four years later. His enthusiasm left in a few days.

Descartes' work on the dream may be anagogic and in the mode of Silberer, but let us not from our twentieth-century vantage point brush off his comments as banal moralizings. It is not unimportant that this great scientist was

struck by a dream, that he quite naturally associated to the elements in it, and that he com-
municated his associations to his friends; and
we should take seriously the judgment he made
on the dream, that it had a prospective tendency
and was a major event in his life, from which
he was to incubate his later convictions.

This brings us to Freud's opinion of the
dream, which was expressed in a letter of a
few hundred words. A French author, Maxim
Leroy, sent him the text and asked for his comments. Freud gently explained that one prefers
to have the dreamer's associations if one must
analyze a dream. He remarked, however, that
the dream was of a familiar type, called a dream
"from above" (*von oben*), that is, one consisting
of ideas that might just as easily have arisen
during the waking state. Such dreams, Freud
continues, most often express abstract, poetic or
symbolic ideas—a remark which suggests that
he too was reminded of Silberer. He states
further that psychoanalysts hearing such a
dream would not be able to interpret it, but
that, on the other hand, the dreamer would
know how to translate it immediately, since the
ideas in it are very near to his conscious
thoughts. Nevertheless, certain elements in such
dreams remain unintelligible to the dreamer

and are to be got at only through free associations from them. "From a certain point of view," he adds, meaning of course the point of view of psychoanalytic theory and genesis, "these are the most interesting details."

Freud, therefore, is willing to accept Descartes' comments as relevant to the interpretation of this dream "from above," and he agrees that it portrays a moral conflict, quite on the surface. The left side stands for sin and the wind is literally an ill wind. Descartes, he is sure, could have identified the persons in the dream, etc. But without more associations to such bizarre elements as the melon from a foreign country and the engravings, one could not get at the deeper unconscious meaning. Descartes' unexpected idea that the melon had to do with the "charms of solitude in a human sense" would make one surmise that it signified sexual material. Freud obviously felt it unwise to be more specific than this, and the letter is written in a restrained style, appropriate to the serious but unsophisticated request. Professor Wisdom, writing in the *International Journal of Psycho-Analysis,* naturally was surer of his readers' critical understanding.

I shall now try to bring together more systematically the ideas which were suggested by the formal aspects of the dream, omitting those that referred to the sexual and moral contents and focusing upon its function as a guardian of sleep. I have assumed that the dream took place during a period of ill health, and I made up a hypothesis of a disturbance in the brain such as usually produces migrainous or convulsive symptoms. The evidence for this assumption was the following: (1) The prodromal intimations, which Descartes reports as present for some days before the dream. (2) The strange sensory and motor images that appeared in the dream; namely, his one-sided paralysis, his spinning around three or four times on his left foot, the feeling of staggering and being bent over, the sensations he interpreted as a high wind, and possibly the "phantoms" he saw at the beginning of the first dream. (3) The sparkling lights in the second dream, inaugurated by the thunderclap and continuing into the waking state, which Descartes states he had experienced many times previously. Although Descartes felt himself to be in violent motion in the first dream and turned from his left to his right side after he awoke from it, it need not follow that he had actually been moving while he was asleep, in the pattern indicated in the dream. Even if the motor phenomena were in fact absent, the symptoms would be intelligible as a so-called "psychic equivalent" of a convulsive or migrainous attack. As to the anamnesis, Descartes' mother died when he was five days old, and his health was the constant worry of his solicitous father and later, from his tenth year on, of the Jesuit teachers to whom his upbringing was entrusted. He spent a large part of his childhood in bed, where his teachers permitted him to stay whenever he wished.

Using the hypothesis just stated, namely, that Descartes was suffering from a physical illness while he was dreaming on the night of November 10, 1619, I shall attempt to interpret certain elements in the dream from the standpoint of its sleep-guarding function and to show how these were used by the dreamer in his effort to preserve sleep. Later I shall try to show that the philosopher's efforts to solve the problem, how may one preserve sleep in the face of intrusive bodily pain and discomfort, have a relationship to his later dualistic picture of the world.

Descartes went to sleep on Martinmas eve, he tells us, quite sober so far as wine was concerned but filled with enthusiasm—inspired excitement—because of his recent intellectual discoveries. But the first dream tries to deal not so much with the wakening effects of thinking;

rather it tries to rid him of physical stimuli by the usual dream process of projecting them as hallucinations. It presents the visual "phantoms" to delude him about any optic impressions and it puts the responsibility for feelings in his body on to a wind. Even so, Descartes' sleep is still threatened. He feels his body very acutely, the hallucinated "wind" makes him stagger, nearly fall; it spins him round, and so the hallucination does not succeed in letting him rest. At this point appears the "threshold phenomenon": he wishes to get away from the wind, that is, his bodily feelings, by taking refuge within the college chapel, where he would be protected and would not feel a wind. The reason he cannot complete this intention in the dream is not clear: the rationalization he gives is that he must turn back to speak to an acquaintance who has greeted him, and whose greeting he has not acknowledged. However, this alternative action and the ensuing conversations with another person and with several others who gather round him, include an attempt to ignore his bodily feelings—an unsuccessful one again, for he is surprised to note suddenly that all these people are standing up perfectly straight and that he alone is reeling and bowed. This surprise we interpret as a new

[41]

failure of the dream work; for if Descartes is to be deluded into thinking that his disturbing sensations are not internal, the dream must see to it that the wind also affects the others. Descartes was philosopher and Bible scholar enough to know that the empirical reality of a wind depends on its blowing on everyone, the just and the unjust alike, and he had to face the fact that it was his body alone that was affected. The dream was unable to project the staggering, painful sensations away from him and on to other persons or on to the physical world. At this point the sleep-preserving mechanisms failed completely and Descartes awoke, discovering the factual nature of his physical discomforts. The failure of the dream to guard his sleep lay in its inability to maintain the delusion that his body was an insentient, nonmotile part of the projected dream picture. A successful dream would, perhaps, have shown him all kinds of phantasms and motions, but it would have permitted him to be present solely with "mental ego feeling," that is, as a detached observer, as an irrelevant spectator.

When through prayer he was able to sleep again, the second dream was an even less effective guardian of sleep. The best it could do by way of hallucination was to depict an internal bodily event as a crash of thunder. Like the waking dream about the "burning child," its illusion lasted a brief moment and Descartes awoke already conscious of the optical phenomena, the sparkles and illumination which he tried to attribute to reflections from objects in the room.

It is too bad that we have no complete record of what went on during this period of wakefulness. We know that there were intense, excited thoughts about what Descartes had just dreamed, by means of which he tried to account for the disturbing events. His thoughts were of sin, of divine illumination, and the like, and they included the moral interpretation; but his thinking must have proceeded in a rapid and complicated fashion and covered many topics. By the time he fell asleep for the third time and began his third dream, as Freud points out, and as Descartes realized, his dreaming intellect carried on the complicated, "abstract, poetic, and symbolic" mentation, which he might just as well have experienced in a waking state, and indeed, which he may well have been experiencing during the waking hours between the dreams, for at the end of the third dream he resumed this style of thinking in what he called his interpretation.

[43]

It seems to me that during the intervening waking hours, the physical processes had subsided, the electrical circuits in his brain had ceased, and Descartes had brought his body to relative rest by the device of diffuse thinking, that took as its content the moral and intellectual problems that he enjoyed. To express this in more psychoanalytic language, though perhaps not very precisely, Descartes had succeeded in becoming much less body ego and much more observing and thinking mental ego.

This he certainly was in his third dream, which was filled with interesting conversation about science, philosophy, inspiration, and poetry, and even about popular books, for according to Professor Smith, the anthology of Latin poets, first published in 1603, appeared in a second edition in 1611. In this dream, Descartes could identify himself with a looking spectator. Professor Wisdom has remarked on the scopophilic quality of the dream, with all its looking at poems and engravings. But if we think of a person as being conveniently and arbitrarily divisible into various parts and functions—such as arms, legs, sensorium, intellect, and the like—then in this dream we could say, Descartes' body is at rest, but his observing and thinking faculties are pleasantly awake.

Now in his interpretation of the dreams,

[44]

which began while he was still asleep, Descartes
continues in an allegorical and anagogical vein.
He is not interested in analyzing the dream, in
our sense; he is not interested in finding repressed memories or conflicts. He is quite content to let his resistances triumph when he
considers the copperplate engravings, for resistances are interesting only to us Freudians
who wish to get at the repressed. Instead, Descartes took the manifest contents of the dream
as a starting point for the sort of poetic, abstract,
and symbolic thoughts that interested him. In
his third dream, his main preoccupation was in
this direction, but the usual dream device of
hallucinatory projection and visual representation successfully protected his sleep.

Long, long before Silberer's idea of using
manifest dream elements to give the start for
allegorical trains of thought, men had realized
this possibility. If there were delusive dreams
that came to us through the gate of ivory, there
were also true dreams that came through the
gate of horn. Possibly it had been noted too that
some of the thinking done in dreams made
sense and was valid when it was checked by later
empirical tests. Yet, with Heracleitos's impreca-
tion loud in their ears throughout the centuries,
most men have been ashamed of what they think
while they are asleep, and if by chance their

dream does come through the gate of horn, they
are apt to be startled. If they dream rationally,
sober men experience an eerie feeling, as if they
had been singled out for some rare dispensation.
Poets are accustomed to the idea of their irra-
tionality and sometimes vaunt it, our fifth Freud
Lecturer, Mr. Trilling, has told us. Perhaps because of this old tradition, Coleridge was ready
to tell that he had dreamed the Kubla Khan
fragment in its final, highly wrought, prosodic
form. Now, from the standpoint of essential
dream theory, which has always taken into account "day thoughts" and secondary elabora-
tion, it hardly matters whether Coleridge put
the poem into its final and esthetically accept-
able form while he was asleep, or whether he
did so after he woke up, while ruminating over
a dream.

The same holds true for scientific inventions
that come while scientists are dreaming. The
story of Kekulé's hexagonal model of the ben-
zene ring is to the effect that the configuration
came to him during a doze:

I sat writing at my textbook, but the writing
did not go at all well, my mind was on other
things. I turned my chair to face the fireplace and
sank into a half-sleep. Again atoms fluttered before my eyes. Smaller groups remained modestly
in the background. My mind's eye, made acute

became Cartesian mind, *res cogitans;* the dream picture became Cartesian matter, *res extensa.* It is desirable in a dream to separate mind and matter; this helps preserve sleep. It was desirable for Descartes also in his philosophy to separate mind and matter, as a preliminary assumption for the understanding of the real world. Whereas we often use the principle that "reality" must correct fantasy, here we find the great philosopher using fantasy to correct common-sense reality.

In formulating his physical science, Descartes proposed the long-abandoned theory of "vortices." Matter, he thought, filled all of space in the form of infinitely divisible particles, and the particles were packed so tightly that one of them could not move without communicating the motion to the rest. To quote Professor Butterfield (p. 132): "This matter formed whirlpools in the skies, and it was because the planets were caught each in its own whirlpool that they were carried around like pieces of straw. . . . Gravity itself was the result of these whirlpools of invisible matter, which had the effect of sucking things down towards their own center." In other words, the whole universe was spinning, and I hazard the conjecture that it was spinning like himself in the dream when the "impetuous

[51]

wind" spun him around three or four times on his left foot. The projected world of physical science was a windy world, isomorphic with the world in his dream, but Descartes as *res cogitans* and with him all cogitating mankind could come to rest.

The real importance of Descartes' dreaming, then, would not—could not—have been the banal moralizing and mystical fantasies, nor his pilgrimage to the shrine of Our Lady of Loreto. Such thoughts and such a ritual were excursions away from the understanding of the message of his dream. They were absurdly incommensurate with the importance he attributed to it. The real consequences of Descartes' dreaming were in precise harmony with his statement, that the Angel of Truth had come to illuminate him, to reveal to him the mathematical nature of the world, for which, as Schrödinger has told us, the separation of mind from matter is the first postulate.

The psychoanalytic literature contains several studies comparing some of Freud's ideas with those of philosophers: Plato, Hobbes, Spinoza, Schopenhauer, Nietzsche, and others listed by Ernst Kris, come to mind. The question, to what extent Freud is a Cartesian, in this general form makes no sense, but we may specifically ask whether the Cartesian split-off, detached observer appears in Freudian theory. I believe, at least twice. Once we find him as the ideal free-associator, metaphorically sitting in a railroad carriage and passively watching the scenery of ideas go by. This free-associator, as I tried to show several years ago, has always partaken of the role of a dreamer, and the relationship with Descartes' metaphysics here is indeed dubious; certainly, it could be plausibly maintained that Freud's relationship to dreams was as intimate as Descartes'. The second time the Cartesian observer seems to appear in Freud's theories is in a more abstract situation, in Chapter VII of the *Interpretation of Dreams*. There (p. 615) he appears as the abbreviation *Cs* for the system Consciousness, which in the psychology of the dream has assigned to it as a role, "only that of a sense-organ for the perception of psychical qualities," analogous to the role which *Pcpt*, the perceptive systems, play in regard to external reality. It is, therefore, the viewer of or spectator at the dream that was processed through the psychic apparatus diagram. It is idle, however, to speculate to what extent Freud was influenced indirectly by Descartes' thinking.

It would be interesting to inquire whether dreams other than those of the ordinary visually depicted type may have led to other and non-Cartesian views on mind and matter. One would like to know what Einstein dreamed, or Leibnitz, or Lao-Tse. We know more about such matters in the nonscientific world, where many saints have been ready to equate the experiences of intensely affective unprojected, nonvisual, blank dreams with direct knowledge of God and the supernatural. In such dreams, the Cartesian observer himself is lost as such. The dreamer does not separate himself as a spectator, but merges himself with the pure feelings of the dream.

However, any such inquiry would take us quite far from the field where the use of regression and of dreams has interested us tonight, that is, the metaphysics of science. Science began with Heracleitos's banishment of the dream. But with Descartes the dream returned to science in disguise, like Oedipus to Thebes, or the repressed to consciousness—and incidentally, to demonstrate to us the uses of regression.

REFERENCES

Ashby, W. Ross (1954), *Design for a Brain*. New York: John Wiley & Sons, Inc.

Burrt, Edwin Arthur (1954), *The Metaphysical Foundation of Modern Physical Science*. Garden City, N. Y.: Doubleday & Co.

Butterfield, Herbert (1949), *The Origins of Modern Science*. London: G. Bell & Sons, Ltd.

Federn, Paul (1926), Some Variations in Ego Feeling. *International Journal of Psycho-Analysis,* 7:434.

Freud, Sigmund (1900), The Interpretation of Dreams. *Standard Edition, 3 & 4*. London: Hogarth Press, 1953.

————(1929), Brief an Maxim Leroy über einen Traum des Cartesius. *Gesammelte Schriften, 12*:403. Wien: Internationaler Psychoanalytischer Verlag, 1934.

Hartmann, Heinz (1950), Comments on the Psychoanalytic Theory of the Ego. *The Psychoanalytic Study of the Child, 5*:78. New York: International Universities Press, Inc.

Kris, Ernst (1952), *Psychoanalytic Explorations in Art*. New York: International Universities Press, Inc.

Kubie, Lawrence S. (1930), A Theoretical Application to Some Neurological Problems of the Properties of Excitation Waves Which Move in Closed Circuits. *Brain, 53*:156.

Robitsek, Alfred (1912), Symbolisches Denken in der chemischen Forschung. *Imago, 1*:83.

Schrödinger, Erwin (1954), *Nature and the Greeks*. Cambridge University Press.

————(1956), On the Peculiarity of the Scientific World-View. In: *What Is Life?* New York: Doubleday & Co.

Silberer, Herbert (1911), Symbolik des Erwachens und Schwellensymbolik überhaupt. *Jahrbuch für psychoanalytische und psychopathologische Forschungen, 3*:621.

Smith, Norman Kemp (1952), *New Studies in the Philosophy of Descartes*. London: Macmillan & Co. Ltd.

Trilling, Lionel (1950), *The Liberal Imagination*. New York: The Viking Press.

Weyl, Herman (1949), *Philosophy of Mathematics and Natural Science*. Princeton University Press.

Winterstein, Alfred (1913), Psychoanalytische Anmerkungen zur Geschichte der Philosophie. *Imago, 2*:175.

———(1929), Motorisches Erleben im schöpferischen Vorgang. *Die psychoanalytische Bewegung, 1*: 299.

Wisdom, John O. (1947), Three Dreams of Descartes. *International Journal of Psycho-Analysis, 28*: 11.

Woods, Ralph L., editor (1947), *The World of Dreams*. New York: Random House. (Prof. Hilprecht's dream, p. 525.)

Bertram D. Lewin, M.D.

Dr. Bertram David Lewin was nominated to give the Seventh Annual Freud Lecture in recognition of his notable contributions to the science of psychoanalysis.

He was born in Victoria, Texas. After receiving his A.B. degree from the University of Texas, he studied at the Johns Hopkins Medical School. His postgraduate training in psychiatry was begun at the Phipps Psychiatric Clinic, where he remained for two years. He devoted the following two years to the study of neurology and neuropathology at the New York State Psychiatric Institute. He obtained his psychoanalytic training at the Berlin Psychoanalytic Institute, at that time a leading center of analytic teaching.

Returning to New York in 1927, he entered the practice of psychoanalysis, and soon became a leading exponent of Freud's teachings, a position he holds to this day. In 1927 he became a member of the New York Psychoanalytic Society, in which he has held several offices, including the presidency. In 1932, he helped to organize the New York Psychoanalytic Institute, at present the largest center of psychoanalytic teaching in the world. He has been actively engaged in teaching ever since the founding of the Institute, and has played a profoundly important role in the education of all its graduates, having given many didactic courses and seminars in addition to conducting personal analyses and individual supervision of physicians in training.

He has been closely identified with the American Psychoanalytic Association, occupying the presidency of that organization during the period 1946-1947. Under its auspices, he is at present conducting a nationwide survey of psychoanalytic education. For many years, he has been an associate editor of *The Psychoanalytic Quarterly*.

Dr. Lewin possesses broad cultural interests. He is an accomplished linguist, with a working knowledge of eight languages, and a high degree of fluency in several of those, in addition to considerable literary gift in his native English.

It is fortunate that such wide gifts have been devoted to the science and practice of psycho-analysis. He is widely known for his theoretical and clinical contributions, particularly for those dealing with affects, the dream, and archaic fantasy life, although every area of analysis has benefited, directly or indirectly, by his origin-ality, his creativeness and his critical powers.

Publications by Dr. Lewin*

1926

Interstitial Gland Cells in the Human Ovary. *Am. J. Med. Sci.,* 171:518

1927

A Study of the Endocrine Organs in the Psychoses. *Am. J. Psychiat.,* 7:391

1928

Histopathology of the Endocrine Organs in Schizophrenia. In: *Schizophrenia.* Proceedings of the Association for Research in Nervous and Mental Diseases, Vol. V. New York: Hoeber

Zur Geschichte der Gewissenspsychologie. *Imago,* 14: 441-446

English: Conscience and Consciousness in Medical Psychology. *Psa. Rev.* 17:20-25

1930

When Adults Tease. *Child Study,* 7:106

German: Warum Kinder von den Erwachsenen geneckt werden. *Z. psa. Päd.,* 4:312-316

* Only the most important publications are listed.

[60]

The Compulsive Character. *Med. Rev. of Rev.*, 36: 191-199

Kotschmieren, Menses und weibliches Über-Ich. *Int. Z. Psa.*, 16:43-56

Spanish: El ensuciarse con materia fecal, la menstruación y el superyo femenino. *Rev. Psicoanál.*, 3:240-253, 1945

1932

Analysis and Structure of a Transient Hypomania. *Psa. Q.*, 1:43-58

German: Analyse und Struktur einer passageren Hypomanie. *Int. Z. Psa.*, 20:74-84, 1934

Spanish: Análisis y estructura de una hipomanía transitoria. *Rev. Psicoanál.*, 4:782-796, 1947

Anal Erotism and the Mechanism of Undoing. *Psa. Q.*, 1:343-344

1933

Obsessional Neuroses. Chapter in: *Psychoanalysis Today*, ed. S. Lorand. New York: Covici-Friede, pp. 219-228; 2nd ed.: New York: Int. Univ. Press, 1944, pp. 199-206

Portuguese: Neuroses obsessivas. In: *A Moderna Psicoanálisis*. Rio de Janeiro: Gerbum Carneiro, 1946, pp. 267-275

The Body as Phallus. *Psa. Q.*, 2:24-47

1935

Claustrophobia. *Psa. Q.*, 4:227-233

Spanish: Claustrofobía. *Rev. Psicoanál.*, 9:123-128, 1952

1937

A Type of Neurotic Hypomanic Reaction. *Arch.*

Neurol. & Psychiat., 37:868-873 (Adolf Meyer Number)

Explorers of the Mind. *Sat. Rev. Lit.,* 16:3-4; Sept. 11

1939

Some Observations on Knowledge, Belief and the Impulse to Know. *Int. J. Psa.,* 20:426-431 (Ernest Jones Number)

1941

Comments on Hypomania and Related States. *Psa. Rev.,* 28:86-91 (A. A. Brill Number)

1945

Gregory Bateson and Margaret Mead: Balinese Character; a Photographic Study. *The Psychoanalytic Study of the Child,* 1:379-388. New York: Int. Univ. Press & London: Imago Publ. Co.

1946

Countertransference in the Technique of Medical Practice. *Psychosom. Med.,* 8:195-199

Spanish: La contratransferencia en la técnica de la práctica medica. *Rev. Psicoanál.,* 4:23-24, 1946

Training in Psychoanalysis. *Am. J. Orthopsychiat.,* 16:427-429

Sleep, the Mouth and the Dream Screen. *Psa. Q.,* 15:419-443; also in: *The Yearbook of Psychoanalysis,* 3:61-74. New York: Int. Univ. Press, 1948

Spanish: El dormir, la boca y la pantalla del sueño. *Rev. Psicoanál.,* 5:180-195, 1947

1948

The Neuroses and Their Accompaniment in Physical Dysfunction. Chapter XV in: *Synopsis of Psycho-*

somatic Diagnosis and Treatment, ed. F. Dunbar. St. Louis: C. V. Mosby, pp. 398-408; 6, 26, 390

The Nature of Reality, the Meaning of Nothing; with an Addendum on Concentration. *Psa. Q.,* 17:524-526; also in: *The Yearbook of Psychoanalysis,* 5: 72-74. New York: Int. Univ. Press, 1950

Inferences from the Dream Screen. *Int. J. Psa.,* 29:224-431; also in: *The Yearbook of Psychoanalysis,* 6: 104-117. New York: Int. Univ. Press, 1951

Spanish: Inferencias sobre la pantalla del sueño. *Rev. Psicoanál.,* 6:330-345, 1948

1949

Child Psychiatry in the 1830's: Three Little Homicidal Monomaniacs. *The Psychoanalytic Study of the Child,* 3/4:489-493. New York: Int. Univ. Press & London: Imago Publ. Co.

Mania and Sleep. *Psa. Q.,* 18:419-433

(& Lawrence S. Kubie) Psychoanalysis (A Supplement to Freud's 1925 article). *Encyclopedia Brittanica,* 18:722-723. Chicago

1950

The Psychoanalysis of Elation. New York: W. W. Norton & Co.; London: Hogarth Press, 1951

Spanish: *Psicoanálisis de la Exaltación.* Buenos Aires: Editorial Nova, 1953

1951

(& Lawrence S. Kubie) Mankind Discovers Man. *N. Y. Evening Post,* 150th Anniversary Edition, Nov. 12; pp. 33-34

(& Henry Alden Bunker) A Psychoanalytic Notation on the Root *GN, KN, CN.* In: *Psychoanalysis and*

[63]